Beluga Sturgeons

by Grace Hansen

Abdo
SUPER SPECIES
Kids

Abdo Kids Jumbo is an Imprint of Abdo Kids
abdopublishing.com

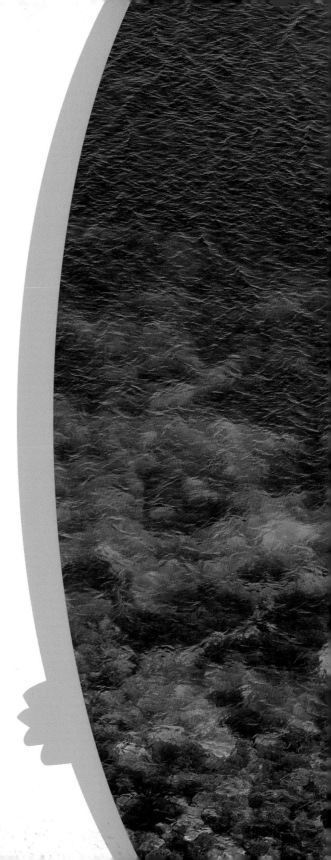

abdopublishing.com

Published by Abdo Kids, a division of ABDO, P.O. Box 398166, Minneapolis, Minnesota 55439.
Copyright © 2019 by Abdo Consulting Group, Inc. International copyrights reserved in all countries.
No part of this book may be reproduced in any form without written permission from the publisher.
Abdo Kids Jumbo™ is a trademark and logo of Abdo Kids.

052018

092018

 THIS BOOK CONTAINS RECYCLED MATERIALS

Photo Credits: Alamy, Getty Images, iStock, Minden Pictures, Shutterstock

Production Contributors: Teddy Borth, Jennie Forsberg, Grace Hansen

Design Contributors: Dorothy Toth, Laura Mitchell

Library of Congress Control Number: 2017960564

Publisher's Cataloging-in-Publication Data

Names: Hansen, Grace, author.

Title: Beluga sturgeons / by Grace Hansen.

Description: Minneapolis, Minnesota : Abdo Kids, 2019. | Series: Super species |
    Includes glossary, index and online resources (page 24).

Identifiers: ISBN 9781532108228 (lib.bdg.) | ISBN 9781532109201 (ebook) |
    ISBN 9781532109690 (Read-to-me ebook)

Subjects: LCSH: Sturgeons--Juvenile literature. | Body size--Juvenile literature. |
    Animals--Size--Juvenile literature. | Animal behavior--Juvenile literature.

Classification: DDC 597.4--dc23

Table of Contents

Big, Old Fish!

Beluga sturgeons are the largest sturgeon . They are also the largest freshwater fish in the world!

5

Beluga sturgeons only spend part of their lives in fresh water. They spend the other part in salt water. They live in the Caspian and Black seas near Russia.

7

These fish can live for more than 100 years. This gives them lots of time to grow.

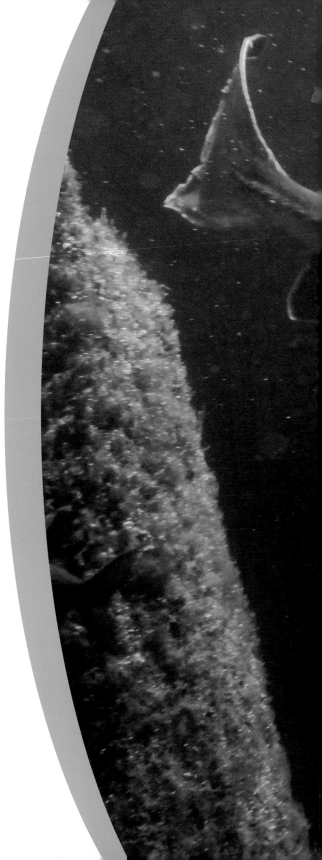

9

Beluga sturgeons can weigh as much as 3,000 pounds (1,361 kg). That is more than some great white sharks!

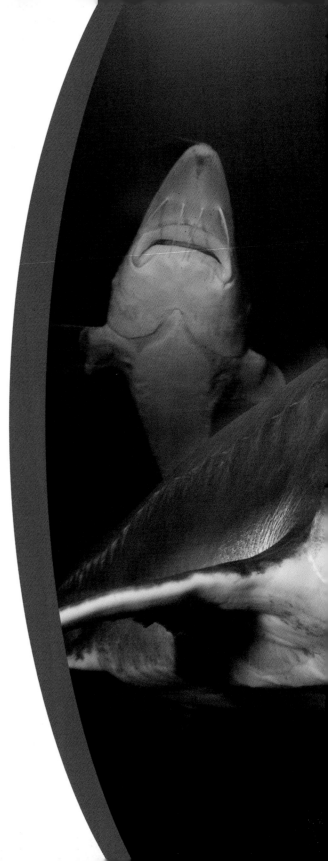

One of the largest beluga

sturgeons ever caught was

23 feet (7.0 m) long. That is

longer than a hammerhead

shark!

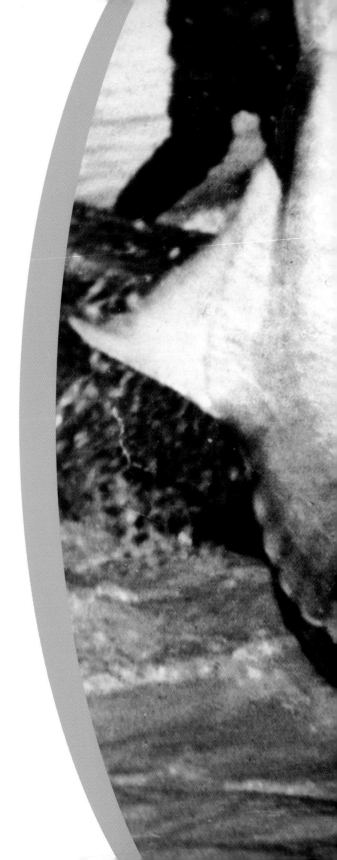

13

Food

A beluga sturgeon has to eat a lot of food. It will eat whatever fits in its big mouth. This includes other fish and **invertebrates**.

Baby Belugas

Adult beluga sturgeons are often ready to **spawn** in spring. They swim back to **freshwater** rivers.

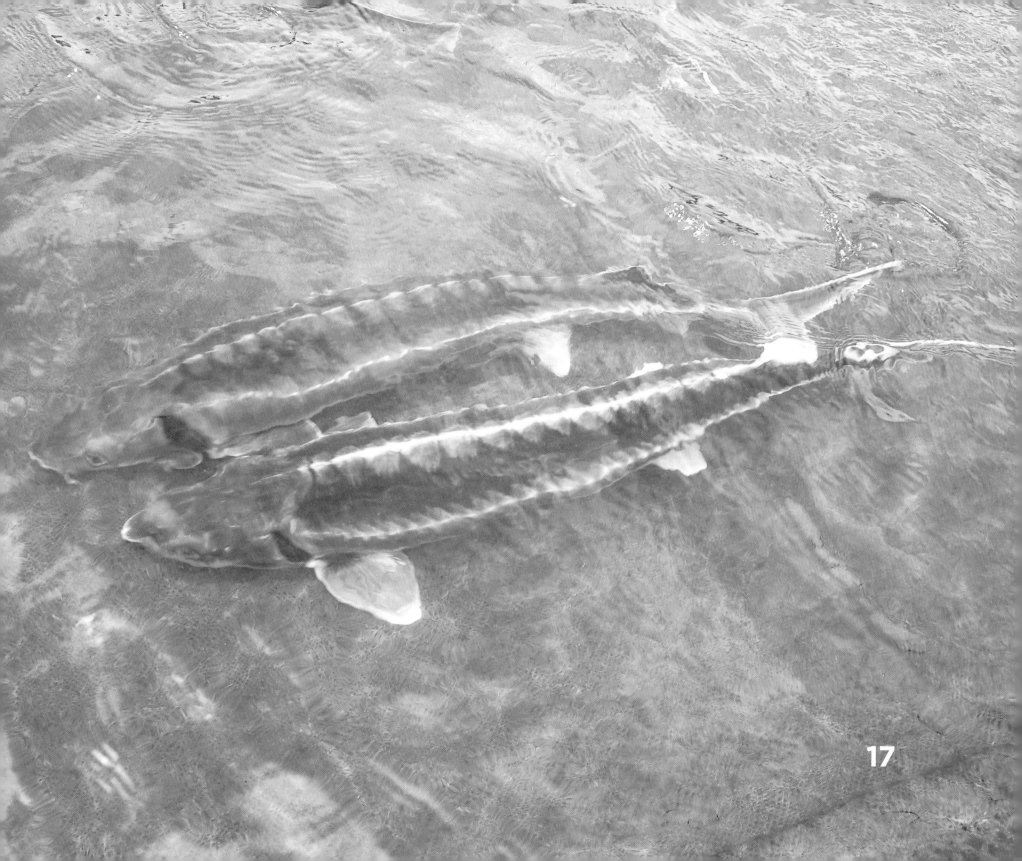

17

Females can lay thousands
of eggs at once. The eggs
hatch after a few days.

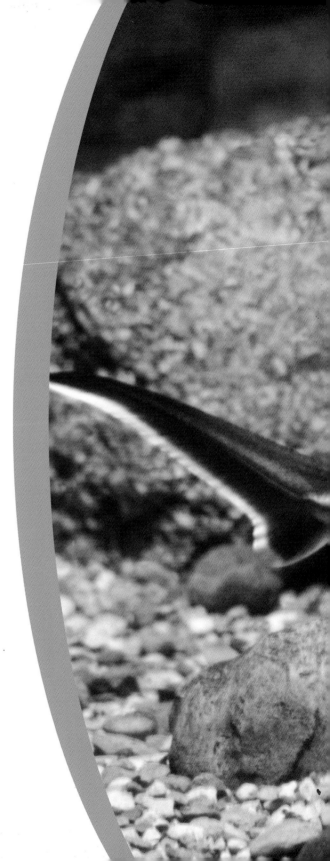

Fry swim toward the sea. They eat along the way. It will take many years for them to be the size of their parents.

More Facts

- Beluga sturgeon are born in **freshwater** rivers. After they are born, they swim to sea. When they are ready, they swim back upriver to **spawn**.

- The average size of beluga sturgeons has gone down. This is because they have been overfished and do not live long enough to grow big.

- Beluga comes from a Russian word that means "white."

Glossary

freshwater – living in water that is fresh or not salt.

fry – a very young fish.

invertebrate – an animal without a backbone.

spawn – to make a large number of eggs.

species – a group of living things that look alike and can have babies together.

Index

Abdo Kids ONLINE

FREE! ONLINE MULTIMEDIA RESOURCES

Visit **abdokids.com** and use this code to access crafts, games, videos, and more!

Abdo Kids Code:

SBK8228